N

MW00795129

USPOCO BOOKS, a non-profit publisher, is a division of us poetry company.

uspocobooks@gmail.com

NIGHT CRADLE
Copyright © 2011 **by Sy Hoahwah**

ISBN 978-0983306214
Library of Congress Control Number:

FIRST EDITION

Cover Photo by Check Ribs

SECTIONS CHAPBOOK SERIES

No. 1

USPOCO BOOKS

Asheville, NC

NIGHT CRADLE

Sy Hoahwah

USPOCO BOOKS

ASHEVILLE, NC

**For
Glen**

I slept beside _____'s grave
until I dreamed. When I woke up
a fox had my skull
on top of his head
praying to the Big Dipper.
The fox looked like a grown person
in the face.
In a greasy voice,
it called me tall meat.
When I was the bones,
carried the saga of the woods in my overalls.
I wrote on the pine needles with pine needles
a line about the life of what was in the way.
My guardian angel stirred the campfire
with a straightened-out wire coat hanger.
Moonlit drops shaken off
the angel's twenty dollar bill
when snakes licked my ears,
I gained prophetic knowledge.
I threw my pocket knife from the previous life.
It still rings from the hilltop covered in clouds.
My discarded clothes had their own hands and feet
and gathered at the fence row
passed themselves off as the stranded
needing a ride
into town.
I dug a hole into the ground
escaping marriage
to the elk scraped moon.

Toward Mount Scott,
it is sharp as a knife.

The bad roads lead to lost roads.
The lost roads lead to the same

empty spot. People sometimes go
to lonely places for power.

Eagles are sometimes choked,
dragonflies lassoed.

Smaller birds follow ghosts
to eat off the bugs.

Line of barbed wire
marks the boundary

between this world
and the next.

Ever since I can remember,
the decapitated head sings

about being
in a brass bucket

at the foot of a cold mountain.
Then it chases us-

lightning
tied to its hair

jagged teeth glow.
Voice sharpened

on the stones
swallowed.

Speed up
slow down

a vengeance
old tribal times.

Lightning has no sympathy
for anyone.

Lightning struck the eye
of the neighbor's dog
while it drank hail water.

Lightning also likes to look
into mirrors.

A woman, feathering her hair,
was struck in the mouth
and killed.

However, my mother's cousin
was best friends with lightning.

She married lightning.
Every time a storm approached
sparks flew from her armpits.

My siamese twin is a boring partner
who insists on helmets.
I want to go to Memphis.
He wants to go to Wind River.

We set out on a bicycle with a banana seat.
We listen for stray dogs, warm rain,
and for the corpse wandering the countryside
who is not ashamed to laugh
with someone else's blood on its teeth.

So focused on listening,
we pedal out to where
moonlight breaks like a knife blade
on the silence.

When I wear my dress shoes,
I find myself wandering aimlessly
like a dream going into the trees.
Or my shoes lead me into perilous situations.
Once, I woke up on the highest point
of the shakiest rooftop.
So close to bumping into the dead,
flower petals fell into my eyes
when their mouths opened
to receive the stars.

What is left

of my family's 160 acres:
A lone pecan tree
on the fringe of Cache Creek.

A squirrel runs up and down
the trunk

carrying insults

between my dead grandfather
and the birds that live

in the top branches.

I carve my name
on the moon's teeth.

When the ice is heavy on the wings
and it's easy to tear the moonlight
out of the trees,
I signal the # of fatalities
by raising and lowering
my black blanket.
My skin
hardened in forge fire.
My genitals
shine like a Ulysses S. Grant peace medal.

Since I can't leave this ghost town,
my job is to blacken things
that need blackened.
Gun holsters,
undertaker's teeth,
church bells,
apple on the schoolmaster's desk
—the orchards have been long gone.
"Disappointment is the best adventure . . ."
exclaims the town's oldest prostitute.

Out of the lake,
we caught a catfish

kept it,
starved it for days.

The fish began speaking
like a human

foretold our futures,

how Death's moustache
is a soft thing

like a kitten

or a wad of cotton.

And for days,
we looked in that fish
for the luck bone.

Catfish's constant smile

moved like a snake
in the water.

Before we are eaten,
the raccoon-witch-cannibal-monk sings to us,
showing rolls upon rolls of teeth.

The songs are always about the Arapaho girl
whose parents' names are White Crazy and Grief
and how she offers her last finger as a sacrifice.

Then the cannibal monk takes a bow,
wearing his own gigantic scrotum as a robe.

At the center of the center of the center of things,
he keeps us. His stomach is a small bedroom
with an old mattress and wooden floor

lined with old newspapers
and coffee cans full of kerosene
for the scorpions that come out to mock.

Night barely fits my house,
her legs lie in one corner,
an arm in an other,
her head underneath the bed.
I lost a tooth
in the hair around night's nipple.
Her nose grows
into the ceiling.
Height of the ceiling devours the lamplight,
no distinction
between the ceiling and the hard surface
of the other world's howl.

9:13 The sun slowly crosses the hair
on the eyepiece of the dead mother coming down
looking around for her children. Horses expand
and contract across a hilltop and empty out
into a valley singed in the grease of strength.
A hornet drifts into a deserted house around the
waist of silence. Underneath the porch, butterfly
wings melt in cat saliva. I keep knocking my face
on the sunlight.

Split
Inverted Press (2001)

Black Knife
Sequoyah Research Center (2005)

Velroy and the Madischie Mafia
West End Press (2009)

32933945R10022

Made in the USA
Middletown, DE
09 January 2019